The Belsay estate as visitors see it today is steeped in more than 600 years of Northumberland's history. Here, perhaps more than anywhere else in the county, visitors can realise and appreciate the continuity and evolving style of life in the borders between England and Scotland. Since the construction of the Castle, in about 1370, there has been continuous occupation by generations of the Middleton family, first in the Castle, then in the Manor House attached to it, and finally in the Hall, until 1962 when Sir Stephen moved out of the Hall to a smaller house nearby.

Each of the three main buildings on the Belsay estate, Castle, Manor House and Hall, is remarkable in its own right and can be rightly recognised as important for its time. The Castle is one of the best examples of the border tower-houses of the fourteenth century. The Manor House, annexed to it, is a Jacobean house, important in that it was one of the first unfortified houses in this area for 300 years or more and its construction heralded a new era of peace. Belsay Hall, in many ways the most remarkable of the three, is one of the highlights of architectural trends in the later Georgian period, which rediscovered and called on the forms of classical architecture for their inspiration and design.

The history of Belsay, however, is more than that of its buildings alone, for the landscape of the estate is also of great interest. Changing fashions in garden layout and design, from at least the seventeenth century onwards, have left their mark. The most obvious elements of this, and those for which Belsay is famous, are the nineteenth-century gardens created around his hall by Sir Charles Monck. The gardens he also created in the quarries, which produced the stone for the Hall and other buildings, were host to a variety of plants, many of them originally from exotic places, collected or selected by Sir Charles and his successors.

Belsay, then known as Beleshou, is first recorded as being in the possession of the Middleton family in 1270, but it is not clear for how long the family had then owned it. In the previous year, Sir Richard de Middleton had become Lord Chancellor at the Court of King Henry III; the first, and perhaps the only, member of the family to hold a high office on a national rather than a local stage. In 1317, however, Sir Richard's successor, John de Middleton, helped to lead an ill-advised northern rebellion against the King, in protest against the insecurity of the borders as a result of the English defeat at the hands of the Scots at Bannockburn in 1314. At the head of a rabble army, more intent it seems on pillage than political protest, John de Middleton and his cousin, Gilbert, marched south. The protest ended with the arrest of the ringleaders, their merciless execution and the confiscation of their lands. For much of the fourteenth century, therefore, the Belsay estate came into the possession of Sir John de Strivelyn.

By about 1370, the estates were back in the possession of a Sir John de Middleton, who may have married into the de Strivelyn family. His son is said to have lived in 'his tower of Belshowe'. The date of the tower's construction cannot be fixed with certainty, but its style suggests that is was probably built in the latter part of the century. An armorial stone, originally on the south front of the Castle but now indecipherable, is recorded as having once borne the arms of both the Strivelyn and Middleton families. The Castle, then called *turris* (tower), was first mentioned in a list of border fortifications made in 1415.

Belsay Castle from the southeast

One of the armorial bearings from the wall paintings within the Castle's main hall

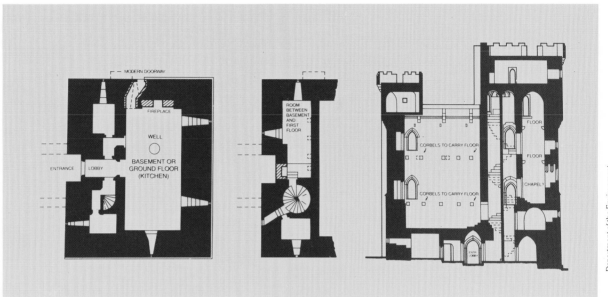

▲
Plans of the Castle at basement and at main hall level, and a cross-section to show the room layout
▼

Department of the Environment

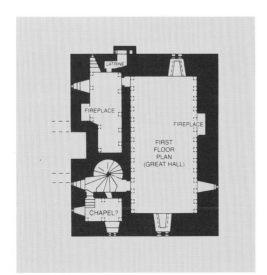

The latter part of the fourteenth century was a time of considerable lawlessness and unrest on the borders between Scotland and England, and it is to this period that the construction of many of the fortifications in the area can be assigned. Belsay Castle is one of the finest of these. It was planned and built with defence in mind, though this was not an overriding priority. Within such a castle as Belsay, which was one of the most elaborate and spacious of its type, all the necessary accommodation for a medieval lord of the manor and his household was fitted. There were main rooms on three storeys: kitchen at ground level, with great hall above, and great chamber above that. Further smaller chambers are found within two short wings that flank the ground-floor entrance. At roof level there are battlements and machicolations, and small circular towers at the four corners. The tower in the southwest corner, which houses the main spiral stair, rises higher above the battlements; there are rooms at six levels within this tower including one, at the level of the great hall, which may have been a small chapel.

The accommodation for the lord was relatively luxurious. As well as the great hall and chamber, there were subsidiary chambers at both main levels, each of them served by garderobe (latrine) shafts. Traces of painted wall-decoration — a relatively rare survival, possibly of early fifteenth-century date — are still to be seen in the great hall. These include shields hung from trees against a floral background, with paintings of sailing ships above. The effect is rather similar to tapestries or wall-hangings, and the painting may have been intended as imitations of these.

Although the Castle, or tower-house, is the only surviving remnant of its date, it may originally not have stood entirely alone. It could, for example, have formed an extension to an earlier hall on the site now occupied by the Manor House, built in 1614. It may also have been linked to a barmkin, or enclosed yard, containing other buildings. Portions of the present buildings around the Castle appear to contain walls that may be of late fifteenth- or sixteenth-century date, and therefore be parts of late medieval additions to the Castle.

In the medieval period the Castle was not isolated in parkland, as it is now; a village settlement grew up around it. This lay along the main route from Newcastle towards Jedburgh, which originally ran just to the south of the Castle. This road was finally diverted round the Belsay estate in the nineteenth century, when the last remnants of the village were also moved outside the gates. The fields surrounding the Castle, at present parkland, contain traces of this settlement, both its system of medieval open fields (ridge-and-furrow) and earthwork remains of the village houses (crofts) and their gardens or yards (tofts). The ruins of a building which may have formed part of this medieval village can be seen in the right foreground of the Buck engraving of 1728 (see pages 4 and 5). The medieval village cross still stands near the Castle, although it has been moved from its original position.

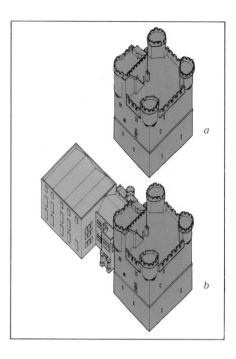

a

b

The Manor House

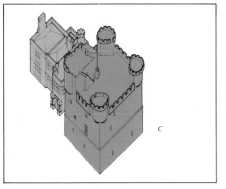

Department of the Environment

▲
◄ *Axonometric views of the Castle and Manor House complex*
a The Castle, c1370
b The Castle and Manor House, c1728
c The Castle, ruined Manor House, and rebuilt dwelling, late nineteenth century

The engraving of Belsay Castle by the Buck brothers in 1728, showing the Castle, central Manor House of 1614 and the large wing (to left) dated to the early years of the eighteenth century
▼

By the early years of the seventeenth century, after the establishment of James as King of Scotland and England, a measure of security was achieved in border areas. For many years cross-border raids and clan or family feuding had been a fact of border life; county authorities had been powerless to curb it. While the accession of James to the throne of England in 1603 did not immediately bring peace, it gave the promise of enough security to enable a country gentleman in this area to improve and civilise his family seat.

At Belsay, Thomas Middleton redesigned his home by adding to the Castle. The original form of his new extension is not certain, but the main front of the House is shown on the Buck engraving of more than a century later. This depicts the Castle to the right, balanced to the left by a large projecting wing with Georgian windows (dated to the early eighteenth century) and linked by a block with mullioned windows and a central projecting porch. This porch and the windows of the central range are probably those visible on the site today, that have survived rebuilding in the Victorian period. Above the porch an inscription in a cartouche records that 'Thomas Middleton and Dorothy his wife built this House anno 1614', and a further inscription records the date 1629.

The date 1614 establishes this new House at Belsay as one of the earliest undefended residences in Northumberland. While this form of construction would not have been at all out of place in the Midlands or southern England for half a century or more, it was novel this far north. Exactly how the House was arranged can now only be surmised, but it is likely that the central porch opened into a hall within the central range. The west wing on the Buck engraving could possibly have belonged to the House of 1614, and have been given a new series of windows just prior to the artists' drawing. It seems likely that by 1728 at any rate, it housed the main staircase and a substantial suite of rooms, counterbalancing, by their lightness and roominess, the rather cramped conditions of the Castle. The medieval Castle may still have been retained as living quarters, but the fact that it was never modernised in Georgian times, according to the standards of the day, shows that the focus of the home was shifting into the newer portions.

In front of the House, the Buck engraving shows a typical formal garden layout, with railings, garden parterres, statuary and clipped topiary trees. It also shows a second walled garden beyond, apparently on a slightly higher terrace, growing fruit, vegetables and flowers. It is hard to equate this with the aspect of the site today. In front of the House is a flat parkland, with only the barest trace of the level garden as shown in the engraving, and a ha-ha wall, created in the nineteenth century, separates the Castle and the remains of the House from the ground in front of it.

▲

Drawing by Swinburne, done in the 1820s, showing the Castle balanced originally by the large west wing

Belsay Castle and Manor House today

▼

 The remains of the House today are fragmentary. Of the large west wing only a small stub of walling survives; a series of sketches from various periods in the nineteenth century, done by members of the Middleton and Monck families, shows the progressive dilapidation of this portion of the House. Only the central portion attached to the Castle survives, and this was remodelled in 1862. At about the same date, doubtless, a series of flowerbeds and the ha-ha wall around the area were created.

Over the course of two centuries, between 1614 and the completion of the new Belsay Hall on its new site, this historic centre of the estate was converted and adapted to become a gentleman's residence. Ancillary buildings were added to the rear, including a fine stable block built probably by 1750, and further outbuildings were added in the nineteenth century. All this was left on one side, however, on the inheritance of the estate by Charles Monck in 1799, as his ambitious scheme for the estate focused on new and totally different plans.

Overall sketch of Belsay Hall, Castle and Gardens
▼

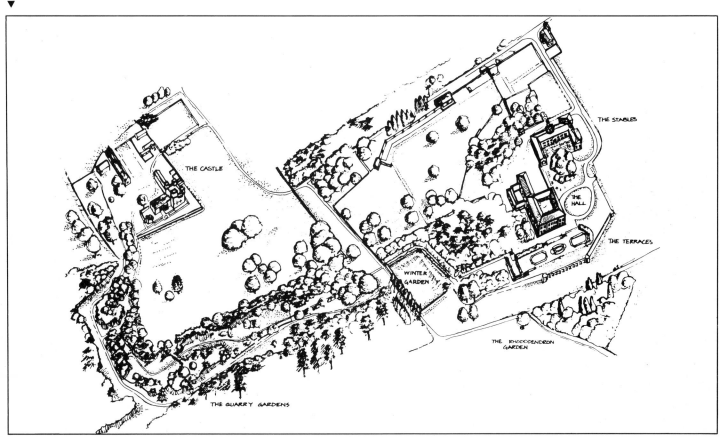

R A Banks

Sir Charles was born in 1779, the son of Sir William and Lady Middleton. As a result of the deaths of his two elder brothers, he was by the age of ten the sole heir to the Belsay estate, and when Sir William died in 1795, he was brought up by his mother who went back to live with her parents, Lawrence and Jane Monck of Caenby in Lincolnshire. On Lawrence Monck's death in 1799, he also inherited the Caenby estate, on condition that he changed his name from Middleton to Monck.

Sir Charles's education was received at Rugby School, where it appears that he was encouraged in two directions which were to have a formative influence on his life and on the Belsay estate in particular. One was the study of Classical languages and literature, in which Sir Charles was a proficient scholar and maintained a lively interest. The other was the development of his talent for drawing. There is no record that he pursued his education at a university or at the Inns of Court, and by 1801 he was back in Northumberland as heir to a considerable fortune.

In September 1804 he married his cousin, Louisa Lucy Cooke of Wheatley Park, Doncaster, and the couple spent their honeymoon abroad in those parts of the Continent not affected by the long war with France. Sir Charles kept a diary of the trip, which lasted about two years from their wedding day. During this time their son, who was named Charles Atticus, was born. From Doncaster they travelled to Harwich, thence to Germany, in particular Berlin.

The architecture of Berlin in 1804 was at a critically formative stage in the German Neo-Classical style. From Sir Charles's diary it is clear that he saw and approved in general of several of the new buildings then going up in the city, and in particular the Brandenburg Gate, built by 1794, which he sketched. The few days spent in Berlin at the start of his honeymoon were to prove an important influence on later events. The Moncks' European tour continued through Dresden, Prague, Vienna, Trieste and Venice, and ended at Athens, where they stayed for a year and where Charles Atticus was born. There Sir Charles studied the greatest examples of classical Greek architecture and also collected a variety of plants. The worsening state of the war with France in 1806 convinced the Moncks that they must return to England, which they did by direct sea voyage in the latter part of that year.

▲
Sketch portrait of Sir Charles Monck, the builder of Belsay Hall

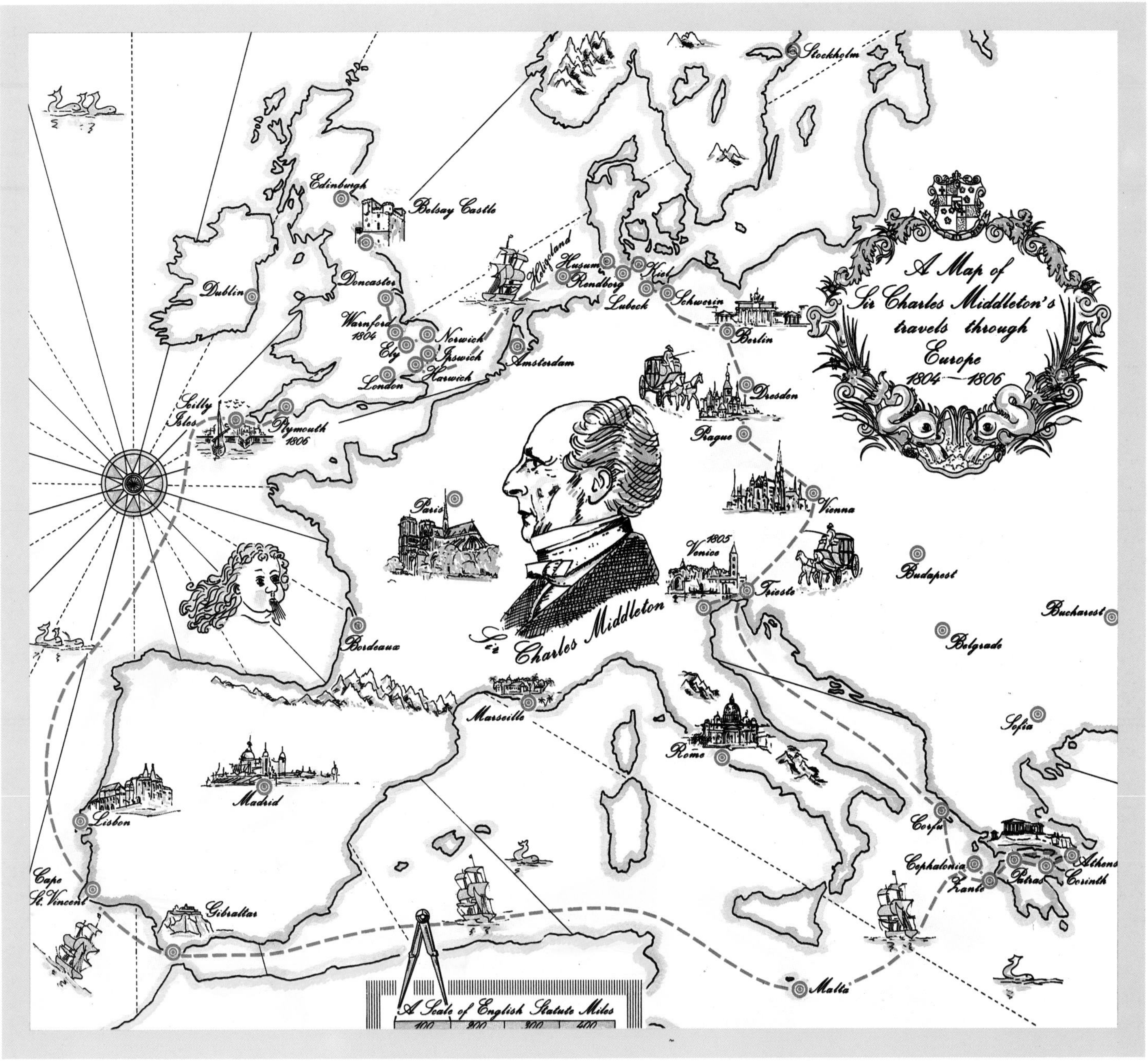

A Map of
Sir Charles Middleton's
travels through
Europe
1804 — 1806

Stockholm

Edinburgh
Belsay Castle
Dublin
Doncaster
Heligoland
Husum
Rendsburg
Kiel
Warnford
1804
Lubeck
Schwerin
Norwich
Ely
Ipswich
Harwich
London
Amsterdam
Berlin
Scilly
Isles
Plymouth
1806
Dresden
Prague
Paris
Vienna
1805
Venice
Budapest
Bucharest
Belgrade
Sir Charles Middleton
Bordeaux
Trieste
Marseille
Rome
Sofia
Madrid
Corfu
Lisbon
Cephalonia
Zante
Patras
Corinth
Athens
Cape
St. Vincent
Gibraltar
Malta

A Scale of English Statute Miles
400 300 200 100

Department of the Environment

▲

The route of Sir Charles and Louise Monck's honeymoon, 1804-06

All this time Sir Charles was planning the design of a new, specifically Neo-Classical, mansion for his family at Belsay. It is likely that all the surviving plans, elevations and detailed drawings, of which there are more than 200, are his own work. He is said to have enlisted the help of John Dobson, the young Newcastle architect who later achieved a great reputation in the northeast, to draw up some of the detail, but the extent of Dobson's input, considering Sir Charles's own talents as a draughtsman, is unclear.

On 25 August 1807 Sir Charles's 'commonplace' book records that 'the foundation of the new house was begun to be dug.' By the middle of August 1815 the masonry, except the fluting of columns of the portico and the staircase, was completed. Building work, including the slating of the roof, was complete by October 1815, but the Moncks and Sir Charles's two sisters did not move into the new Hall for another two years.

The design of the Hall owes much to the influence of the Classical buildings that Sir Charles had seen, drawn and studied while in Greece, and also, perhaps to a lesser extent, to German Neo-Classical architecture of the 1790s. In plan, the building is a perfect square of 100ft (30m), and all dimensions are worked out on the plans to the minutest accuracy.

Nineteenth century view of Belsay Hall
▼

Only on the north side, where the kitchen wing and service courtyard lie, is this four-square symmetry interrupted. The house is built of honey-coloured stone, which contains flecks of iron, taken from within the quarry in the gardens. The site chosen for the house was that of a prominent knoll to the southeast of the Castle and Manor House, partly occupied by a chapel belonging to the medieval village.

In the east front is the entrance, which is dominated by a massive pair of fluted Doric columns that guard the main entrance doors, like the portico of a Greek temple. The whole edifice rises from a massive stepped plinth that runs all the way round the building. The façade of the building to the left and right of the entrance is in plain smoothly dressed stone, punctuated by four regularly spaced engaged pilasters between which are symmetrically spaced windows on two storeys. Above the entrance columns and engaged pilasters there is a Doric entablature with a projecting cornice, which, on the right day, casts a deep and striking shadow along the topmost portion of the building.

The other two fronts — the main elevation overlooking the gardens to the south and that looking out on the woodland area to the west — show the same striking severity of design. The fronts are strictly symmetrical and they use the same themes of plain Doric engaged pilasters and two storeys of windows with plain surrounds. Above all this runs an entablature and cornice. The roofs are of so low a pitch that they are difficult to see except from a distance.

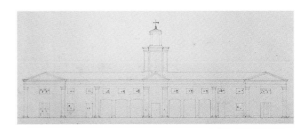

▲

Two of the original plans for Belsay Hall and stables, drawn by Sir Charles Monck

The entrance front of Belsay Hall
▼

Northumberland Record Office

National Monuments Record

Internally the layout is simple. From the portico visitors first enter the entrance hall, and through this arrive in the pillar hall, which in its central position within the house, is an attempted reconstruction of the central courtyard of the Greco-Roman house. At ground-floor level, most of the main rooms open off this central hall, which is lit from above and is surrounded by columns on two storeys, Ionic on the ground floor and Roman Doric above.

At first-floor level, the spaces between the columns were adorned with brass grilles in ornate style. The largest room in the house is the library, set centrally in the south front and lit by four massive windows. Like all the other rooms its internal detail — here the bookcases, plasterwork and fireplace of yellow imitation marble and white stone — was minutely planned and finely finished. The room is at present unfurnished, but it once contained elegant mahogany and rosewood Regency furnishings, as well as the Middleton family's large collection of books. Other rooms on the ground floor include Sir Charles's study, and, on the south front at either end of the library, the drawing room and the dining room. On the upper floor, a similar plan to that on the ground floor is maintained by the extension of the central open space of the hall up to the roof. Bedrooms and bedroom corridors, arranged in suites, open off the landing. Here, too, there is carefully considered detail of friezes and woodwork, and many of the rooms, though now bare of furniture, retain wallpaper of late nineteenth-century date.

The service quarters, which occupy the northernmost third of the house, are extensive. As well as the original kitchen range and courtyard, which project from the ground floor, there are servants' rooms at three levels on the northern side of the Hall, corresponding with the two storeys in the main part of the house. There are further rooms occupying the whole of the roof space, lit from windows facing the central light space to avoid disturbing the austere design of the main façades. The service quarters also afford access to a series of wine cellars deep under the main house.

Country Life

▲
▲
Detail of one of the upper columns in the pillar hall

▲
The pillar hall

The library, as furnished in the 1930s

▲

The stable block, from the front of the Hall

Northeast of the Hall stands the stable block. This reflects the design of the Hall in its use of the same stone and the same distinctive features of engaged Doric pilasters and plain window surrounds. The clock tower at its centre is based on the Tower of the Winds at Athens. To the north of the stables lie the kitchen gardens and paddocks, the site of greenhouses and heated or 'hot' walls against which Sir Charles planted and grew tender fruit trees and in which he grew exotic plants with considerable success.

Sir Charles's new Hall at Belsay is one of the landmarks of later Georgian reawakening of interest in the architecture of Classical antiquity. It was the first house the design of which was based on the domestic architecture of the ancients. Belsay is particularly remarkable, however, within the range of Neo-Classical buildings, for its mathematical exactitude and proportions, for the severity and restraint of Sir Charles's designs and for the precision of their execution.

▲
View south from the Hall terrace, over the rhododendron garden

 The parkland at Belsay slopes gently upwards to higher ground at its western edge. At this point, which commands extensive views, there is an earthwork, commonly referred to as a Roman camp, but which is probably of slightly earlier date, belonging to the Iron Age.

The site chosen for the Castle was less exposed, particularly from the prevailing southwesterly winds, though it still held wide command of the surrounding area. The site of gardens or yards belonging to the Castle cannot now be made out, but the medieval village settlement attracted to the Castle and manorial seat sprawled mainly along a main route leading from east to west through the centre of the present park, just south of the Castle. Around and to the north of the Castle, the presence of ridge-and-furrow preserved in the grassland suggests that medieval open fields once existed there.

After the Manor House had been added to the Castle in 1614, more conscious efforts were made to improve the setting. Trees were planted in the parkland, and during the early part of the seventeenth century more substantial belts of woodland were also planted along the crags, including Bantam Wood to the west of the Castle and Manor House, by Sir William Middleton, third baronet. Snowdrops were planted in the woods by his wife.

The engraving of Belsay Hall produced by the Buck brothers in 1728 shows the Castle and Manor House flanked and fronted by formal gardens. A pair of large iron gates opened out to the south and the gardens were enclosed by walls and railings.

The ferme ornée (known as Bantam Folly), built by Sir William Middleton about 1757
▼

 Throughout the eighteenth century, the parkland evolved round the Castle, mainly under the impetus of Sir William Middleton, fifth baronet, between 1769 and 1795. His improvements included the building of Bantam Folly (the *ferme ornée*) west of the Castle and the new serpentine drive from the north. This drive meandered through the park, presenting the grandeur of the Castle in an appropriate style. It crossed a newly formed lake by a new stone bridge. Many of these improvements were shown on an ambitious plan drawn up by Robson in 1792.

Much of the landscape to be seen today is the product of Sir Charles Monck (1795–1867) and his grandson, Sir Arthur Middleton (1867–1933), who succeeded him. Even before the design and construction of his new Hall, between 1807 and 1817, Sir Charles had begun to collect plants, beautify the gardens and plan the eventual layout of the quarries and the gardens within them. As a setting for his new Hall, he planned a major series of alterations and improvements to the estate and its parkland. Many of the earlier and medieval features including the village and chapel were swept away to provide a more suitable setting for the Hall which was carefully sited. Belsay Lough, the lake to the east of the Castle, was enlarged but after vociferous complaints from the newly settled villagers it was never flooded. The boat house stranded in the field can still be seen from the drive to the north. A new lake was created southeast of the Hall and trees were planted along the Craig Heugh. Substantial terraces were built to the south of the Hall, which emphasised the height of its setting.

The stable building is sited so that it protects the Hall from cold northeasterly winds. The remains of the medieval chapel and graveyard, now covered in birch trees and ivy, separate the Hall from the stables. The gravel driveway was deliberately sunk so that, as visitors drove across the parkland and passed the lodge with its miniature Classical façade, the Hall was seen rising directly above the lawns with no interruptions to detract from the severity of its façade.

▲

*The quarry garden, seen from the path
leading to the Castle*

◄ *Sir Arthur Middleton, who inherited Belsay
in 1867 and died in 1933*

Beginning with the terraces surrounding the Hall itself, the gardens lead westward from the main area in front of the building as a series of contrasting separate areas, culminating in the gardens created in the quarries.

The quarry garden is in complete contrast to the Hall. The Hall is carefully executed, meticulously planned and studied, the very essence of regularity of form and the strictness of Classical architectural design. The quarry, however, in its way no less carefully planned, is of unfinished rock, garnished with plants which soften, accentuate and breathe life into the bare walls over which they climb. This design shows to admirable effect the twin sides of the character of Sir Charles Monck, a man who, as scholar as well as romantic, was able to create both divergent elements in the Belsay landscape. Sir Charles's successors retained the main features of the garden he planned, while adding elements of their own. Sir Arthur Middleton, in particular, created an additional quarry garden when he extracted more stone, and additions and alterations to other minor areas of the gardens were carried out from time to time. Upkeep of the gardens proved difficult after 1945, as during the Second World War the estate had been in military hands and the gardens had not been properly maintained.

▲
The winter garden

◄ *Belsay Hall, the terrace garden, from a
nineteenth-century watercolour view*

When Sir Charles Monck designed and built the terrace, the wide platform stretched from the eastern wall to the farm track. This bold design was broken up by Sir Arthur when he added the hedges sheltering the rose garden and magnolia terrace and the tall wall enclosing the winter garden. The remains of Sir Charles's design can be seen in the formal stone-edged flowerbeds that probably contained colourful annuals. Sir Arthur planted them with shrubs and plants affording ground cover, including *Magnolia × thompsoniana* and *watsonii* and many larger shrubs growing along the wall. Below the terrace to the south, the **rhododendron garden** was established from 1860 onwards on rough ground covered by broom. The rhododendrons, mainly early hardy hybrids, were the foreground to the lake and Craig plantation beyond.

At the west end of the terrace, Sir Arthur planted a Lawson cypress hedge in order to protect the tender young yew in 1909. This area is now the **rose garden** which contains *Rosa iceberg* surrounded with *Alchemilla mollis* and *Hosta plantaginea alba*.

Originally the path heading through the **magnolia terrace** was edged with two long borders of which only one now remains. A large *Magnolia acuminata* (the cucumber tree) grows on the southern edge of the terrace and the rare *Magnolia fraseri*, with its large auriculate leaves, stands on the lawn.

The **woodland** behind was planted by Sir Charles with Scots pine and beech. The rhododendrons and laurels were added by Sir Arthur. These provide shelter from the north winds as well as an evergreen backdrop of pines, their dark foliage contrasting strongly with the mellow colour of the Hall.

◄ *Magnolia sieboldii*

▲
The quarry garden, looking eastwards

The **winter garden** is so called because Sir Arthur interpreted his ideas on labour-saving and colourful ground-covering plants by planting it with winter-flowering heaths and heathers. He also built the tall stone wall that once protected two tennis courts and a croquet lawn. The ha-ha originally ran along the wall dividing the borders from the lawn and in the northeastern corner is a Douglas fir tree, *Pseudotsuga menziesii,* planted by Sir Charles in 1830.

A small door leads across the farm track to the **quarry gardens** and on the left the woodland of Nootka and Lawson cypress, the pyramidical shapes of which are visible above the stone wall from within the winter garden.

Two large beech trees planted by Sir Charles mark the entrance to the quarry gardens. The path leads through a hedge of *Gaultheria 'shallon'* past the large-leaved *Aralia chinensis* (the Chinese angelica tree) and the white-stemmed bramble.

As the stone was cut from the quarry to build the Hall, Sir Charles designed the face to make a picturesque garden. He emphasised the height of the cliffs by planting a dark yew hedge along the top. He listed over twenty-eight species of hardy ferns in 1854 and noted a wide range of wild flowers growing there.

The **meadow garden** full of wild flowers is surrounded by unusual trees. To the south there are several *Parrotia persica* with flaking bark and brilliant autumn colour. Opposite there are two *Magnolia kotus* covered with white flowers in April, a large *Halesia carolina* (the snowdrop tree) the branches of which are draped with white bells in May or early June and a magnificent *Davidia involucrata* (known as the pocket handkerchief tree because of its large white bracts).

Davidia involucrata (the pocket handkerchief) ▶

◄ *The quarry garden in flower*

Glimpses of colour in the quarry
▼

At the end of the meadow garden the quarry face narrows in on both sides to form a dark enclosure. On the south side grows a large *Entianthus campanulatus,* with its cluster of whitish bells, planted in 1908. On the north side is a rare conifer, *Fitzroya cupressoides* from Argentina, and near by is the white-flowered *Eucryphia glutinosa.* Before the arch is a small pond fed by a channel cut into the rock. It is surrounded by species rhododendrons and a tall palm tree, *Trachycarpus fortunei,* grows in a sheltered corner, its stem protected by its dying leaves.

Through the stone arch, the quarry opens out into a second meadow which is edged with more species rhododendrons, including five examples of *campylocarpum* and *thomsonii* and types with small delicate flowers, rust-coloured velvet leaves, or peeling red-cinnamon bark. Ahead is a large pinnacle of rock, now totally covered with ivy, and to its north another island covered with the brilliant autumn-colouring vine *Vitis coignetiae* and a large *Magnolia sieboldii* with its white flowers hanging over the rock face in July.

The path winds round past the well into a dark narrow gorge to end at a wooden door. Through this one emerges into more light and a gently sloping ascent from the Stygian gloom to the Castle and Manor House.

Within the western quarry, two unusual oaks, *Quercus cerris variegata* and *Quercus rubra,* mark the path; there are views across to what remains of the Bantam Folly. The original road leads off into the woodland as the return path descends into the secondary quarry from which Sir Arthur extracted stone for the refurbishment of the Manor House and other buildings.

The stone wall of the eighteenth-century garden hangs over the cliff, and one side of a well, bisected by the quarry, can still be seen in its western face. Amongst the wild flowers and ferns grows the small creeping golden saxifrage, *Chrysosplenium oppositifolium,* which contributes much to create the impression of wildness, admired by Sir Charles and the picturesque school of the late eighteenth century.

Around the car-parking area is the working side of the Hall, from the kitchen wing to the outbuildings, from the paddocks where the horses grazed to the kitchen gardens built by Sir Charles. Here he grew many unusual exotics including bananas, guavas and citrus fruit as well as a supply of vegetables for the house.

This is a thomsonii species from the rhododendron garden ▶

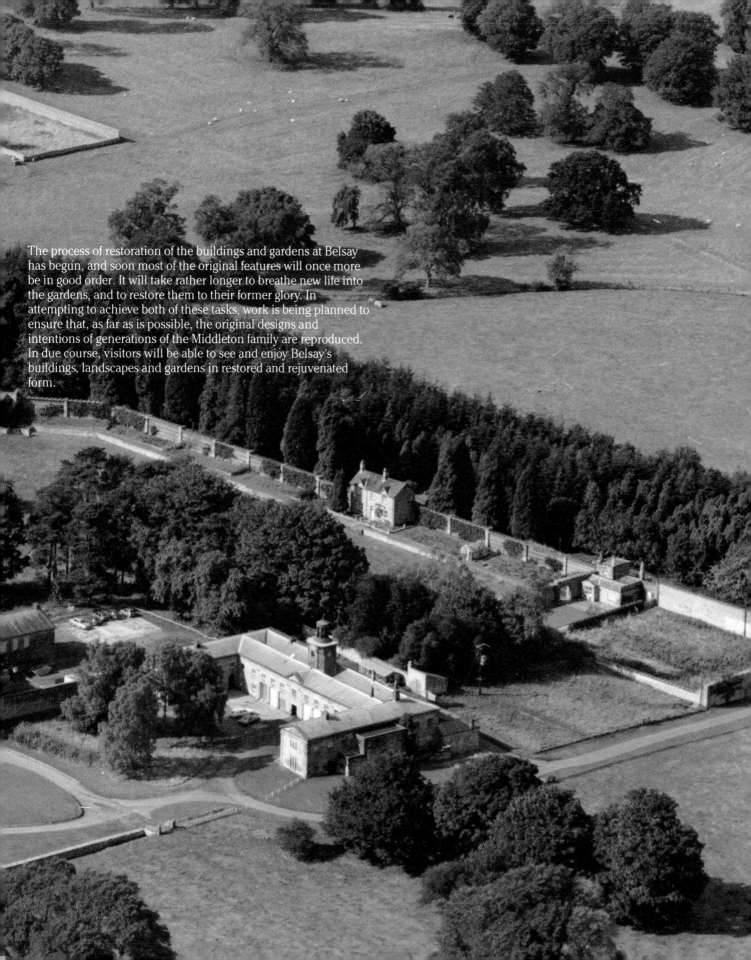

The process of restoration of the buildings and gardens at Belsay has begun, and soon most of the original features will once more be in good order. It will take rather longer to breathe new life into the gardens, and to restore them to their former glory. In attempting to achieve both of these tasks, work is being planned to ensure that, as far as is possible, the original designs and intentions of generations of the Middleton family are reproduced. In due course, visitors will be able to see and enjoy Belsay's buildings, landscapes and gardens in restored and rejuvenated form.